MW01634932

SATAN'S PLAYBOOK

Identifying and Defending Against Satan's Temptations

Jason B. Watson

CrossBooks™
A Division of LifeWay
1663 Liberty Drive
Bloomington, IN 47403
www.crossbooks.com
Phone: 1-866-879-0502

First published by CrossBooks 5/25/2011

ISBN: 978-1-6150-7877-6 (sc)

Library of Congress Control Number: 2011930075

Printed in the United States of America

This book is printed on acid-free paper.

For Cassidy and Owan

Contents

Acknowledgements

I "discovered" the main points of this book during a time of personal Bible study in my senior year of college. I can still see clearly in my mind my dorm room, and remember as though it were yesterday the excitement of having these principles revealed to me.

Since that time I have been privileged to share the realities of Satan's Playbook with hundreds of young people in chapel services and devotionals. I am pleased to have this opportunity to share them with a wider audience now, and it is my prayer that these principles will help each reader recognize and defend against the plays that Satan sends their way.

I am grateful to Kristina for reading through various drafts of this book and offering suggestions, critiques and encouragement. I am blessed to have a wonderful, godly wife, and I cannot imagine tackling this book, or anything else life sends my way, without her by my side.

Dr. Joey Anthony has been a faithful friend, encourager and model in living the Christian life. I was blessed to sit under his teaching as a member of Midway Baptist Church for six years and I appreciate him reading through the draft of this book and offering his feedback.

Rev. Mark Snodgrass provided a thorough review and critique of the draft of this book, and the final version owes much to his careful editing, suggestions for improvement, and identification of my own habits as a writer that I could never pick up on myself. Thanks for helping me "murder my darlings," Mark.

Finally, Kathy Shaibani provided invaluable editing services, and if any reader finds this book to be well-written, Kathy deserves no small part of the credit.

Introduction

When I was growing up, baseball was my favorite sport. Still is, in fact. But, like many kids, I played sports with the kids in my neighborhood, and usually we would change sports with the changing of the professional sports seasons: in spring and summer we would play baseball, in fall we shifted to football, and after football we played basketball. Sometimes these would overlap a little bit, and sometimes it depended on how many players we could round up on any given day. Playing football with just three people is kind of tough, so on those days we would play basketball.

As far as organized team sports, though—Little League, park and rec leagues, and so forth—I played baseball from the time I was five (tee ball counts, right?) until I was in high school. I played on a basketball team for one season, and a flag football team for two seasons. One year in flag football I was the quarterback. My dad was the coach, and every Saturday before a game he would wrap my wrists in athletic tape and then use a black Sharpie to write out the names of the plays that he wanted me to use and the order in which he wanted me to use them. (Quarterbacks in the NFL and NCAA still use this principle, but their wristbands are fancy ones with plastic covers over the plays that the coach wants them to use all typed out). When we went into a huddle I would look at my wrist and call a play, and then we would hustle up to the line of scrimmage and give it our best shot. I can still remember some of those plays today.

Imagine for a moment that you are a member of a football team, and you have the biggest game of the season—maybe even of your career—coming up next Friday. Of all the things that you could do to prepare for that game, what one thing would give you the greatest possible advantage over your opponent? Practicing, getting enough sleep, reviewing game tapes, scouting the other team—all of that would be good. All of that would be fair, too. But what if somehow you had the other team's playbook? If you could go into the game knowing exactly what plays the other team was going to run, wouldn't you have a huge advantage? There would really be no excuse for you *not* to win the game. Of course, just knowing the other team's plays will not necessarily result in a win. Knowing the plays and knowing how to defend against them are two very different things. But any team that knows the other team's playbook will spend their practice time before the big game developing specific defensive strategies—where to block, which receivers to cover, when to blitz, what fakes to watch out for, and so on. Armed with the knowledge of the other team's plays and the skill necessary to defeat those plays, they would go into the game prepared to win.

Now think about how this applies to your Christian walk. We're engaged in spiritual warfare every day, and Satan has standard "plays" that he will run against us, just like a football team has standard plays that their offense will run. And even though Satan has been around for a long time, he has not changed his plays. He may set them up differently—for example, he may use more deception sometimes, or give things a flashier look. But when you get right down to it, Satan tempts us in the same way that he tempted Eve in the Garden of Eden and Jesus in the wilderness, and everyone in between and since. In the Bible we see Satan's playbook. Through His inspiration of the Bible writers, God has provided us with access to the tricks Satan will use. But the Bible even goes beyond that: it provides us with the defense we need to use against Satan's plays. In other words, not only do we have the other team's playbook, but we have instructions on exactly how to set up our defense *from Someone who has already beaten the other team*!

In this book we will look at what the Bible has to say about the tricks and plays that Satan will use, and what we can do to overcome temptation when it comes our way. And it *will* come our way! We'll face temptation every day for the rest of our lives. The funny thing is, Satan—as smart as he is—never develops any new plays. He keeps running the same plays over and over, day after day, year after year. Why does he do that? Again, think about football: If a coach runs the same plays again and again it's because they're *working*. And that's what has been happening for thousands of years—Satan's plays, by and large, have been working, simply because most people don't take the time to figure out what plays he's going to run and how best to defend against them. But those plays don't have to work on you! If you take the time to recognize the plays and learn how to defend yourself against them, you can be victorious!

Two notes of caution before we get into the playbook. First, we will not defeat Satan every time. I am not suggesting that there is a foolproof way to never sin again. The truth is that we *will* be beaten by Satan's plays. Sometimes we'll forget to employ the defense that we practiced; sometimes we'll intentionally not defend against Satan's plays, thinking that the play won't work anyway, or wanting to see what will happen. Sin will not disappear from our lives. The foundational principles in this book came to me during my senior year of college. I've developed these ideas more fully since then, shared this message with hundreds of young people, and endeavored to employ these defenses against Satan's plays—yet I still sin. I will continue to sin until the day I die. But as I grow in grace I should sin less today than I did yesterday, and less last month than last year. As we all continue to grow in God and to trust the defenses He has given us, we will be increasingly victorious over sin in our lives.

Secondly, the defenses described in this book are only effective for Christians. A non-Christian cannot use the defensive strategies revealed in the Scriptures to defend himself against Satan's temptations in his life. If you do not know Jesus Christ as your personal Savior, then nothing in this book will work for you. It can't. To use the football analogy again, it doesn't do you any good to know the plays the other team will run if you aren't even in the game. By the same token, an unbeliever is not on God's team, and consequently he can't play the game using the defenses God has provided. If you have not asked Jesus Christ to be your Savior I would encourage you to read this book anyway. In fact, the very last part of the book is just for you. It is my prayer that this book might reveal to you your need to accept Christ and join His team. God would love to have you!

Jason Watson
Christiansburg, VA
March 2011

SATAN'S PLAYBOOK

Identifying and Defending Against Satan's Temptations

Then Jesus was led up by the Spirit into the wilderness to be tempted by the devil. And after fasting forty days and forty nights, he was hungry. And the tempter came and said to him, "If you are the Son of God, command these stones to become loaves of bread." But he answered, "It is written, 'Man shall not live on bread alone, but by every word that comes from the mouth of God.'"

Then the devil took him to the holy city and set him on the pinnacle of the temple and said to him, "If you are the Son of God, throw yourself down, for it is written, 'He will command his angels concerning you,' and 'On their hands they will bear you up, lest you strike your foot against a stone.'" Jesus said to him, "Again it is written, 'You shall not put the Lord your God to the test.'"

Again, the devil took him to a very high mountain and showed him all the kingdoms of the world and their glory. And he said to him, "All these I will give you, if you will fall down and worship me." Then Jesus said to him, "Be gone, Satan! For it is written, 'You shall worship the Lord your God and him only shall you serve.'" Then the devil left him, and behold, angels came and were ministering to him.

Matthew 4:1-11

Chapter 1

Play #1: Temptation with the Possible

Satan reveals his playbook to us during his temptation of Christ in the wilderness of Israel. The Holy Spirit led Jesus Christ into the wilderness for forty days of fasting. Fasting is the deprivation of the body of food, and sometimes water, in order to focus completely on God and His provision for us. While fasting still has merit today as a spiritual discipline, it must be done properly and with correct understanding of how and why to do it. But here Christ had been in the wilderness for more than a month, and He had had nothing to eat or drink. You can understand, then, why He would be very hungry and thirsty when Satan approached Him.

Satan shows up in verse 3 of Matthew 4, and says to Jesus, “I know You’re hungry. If You really are the Son of God, why not just turn those rocks right there into bread so You can have something to eat? After all, what good is it to have the power that You have and not even be able to get Yourself something to eat?”

Did you catch Satan's first play? He just ran it right in front of you. It's been working against Satan's opponents ever since he played his very first game. It's called *temptation with the possible*, and it is both deceptive and effective. Let's break it down so we can see exactly how it works.

There is no doubt that Jesus was genuinely hungry. He'd just gone almost a month and a half without food. Because He was completely human, He would have felt the same hunger pangs that we do (only more severe). Jesus was very vulnerable at this point, so Satan offered a solution to Jesus' problem. He made it seem so simple—"You're hungry, You've got the power to provide food for Yourself, why not do it?"

This move is effective because it can exploit both desires and needs. In this particular case, Jesus truly needed physical nourishment after His forty-day fast. Satan today may focus on something that we really need—perhaps a new pair of shoes, or a good grade on a test. But sometimes he plays to our desires, such as the coolest name-brand clothing, the flashiest jewelry, or the latest video game. Either way—needs or wants—Satan targets something appealing. Jesus would not have been tempted in the least, for example, if Satan had approached Him and said, "You look as though You could really use a nice new toolbox. Why not turn that stone into one?" Why not? Because Jesus neither needed nor wanted a toolbox at that moment; a toolbox would not have satisfied His physical needs.

There were times in my life when I would have liked very much to have the new G.I. Joe action figure or the newest style in sunglasses. At this stage of my life (obviously, I hope!) those things do not appeal to me. However, there are things I'd like to have now that would never have crossed my mind when I was eight years old (or twelve, or eighteen). Our needs and our wants change.

Unlike God, Satan is not omniscient. *Omniscient* is a big, fancy word that means "all knowing." God knows everything about everyone. The Bible tells us that God knows the number of hairs on our heads—probably a much higher number for you than it is for me!—and that He knows when a sparrow falls from the sky. God is never caught by surprise; He never says "I didn't see that coming." (Of course this also means that we can't hide anything from God or keep any secrets from Him. It just isn't possible). But Satan does not have God's power and knowledge so he's had to learn by observation over thousands of years. He knows what kinds of things tempt young men and young women, young adults and older people. He knows that some things have a stronger appeal to some people than to others. And, above all, he is persistent. If he tries something and it doesn't work, he will try again with a different temptation. That's why part of our defense against this play is being aware of our individual needs and desires and how they change.

This play is also deceptive because it usually offers a possible solution, such as bread, to a real problem, such as Jesus' hunger. Usually when Satan runs this play he is offering us a way to get what we need or what we want. We can be so focused on meeting that need that we miss the danger involved.

In a sense, Satan is much like an angler playing his lure. The fish sees the lure floating in the water, and needs to eat. Focused on how attractive the bait looks and imagining how good it will taste, the fish fails to notice the hook and the line. The fish bites and suddenly feels pain as the fisherman yanks upward on the line, embedding the hook into the fish's mouth. The angler reels in the line, and the fish goes from savoring a tasty snack to wondering how much longer it will live. Satan works just like that—he's always looking for ways to catch us on his hook and reel us in.

So where does the "possible" part come in? Simple—Satan will *always* tempt us with something that is possible for us to do. It may be simplistic in this instance to look at temptation with the possible since we are looking at a situation in which Jesus Christ was the one being tempted, and all things were possible for Him, but this principle holds true for us as well. Satan tempted Jesus to do something that was well within His ability to do—turn stones into bread. Why, then, would it have been wrong for Christ to yield to that temptation? Because He would have been distorting and perverting His divine power to fulfill His own desires (see James 4:3).

Now, if someone—even Satan himself—came to you or me and said "Why don't you turn those stones into bread?" we would not be tempted, because there is no way we could accomplish such a feat. No matter how hungry we might be or how hard we might try, we are incapable of turning stones into bread. And while he is not all-knowing, Satan is smart enough to know what we can and cannot do, and smart enough to know that we will not be tempted to do something that is impossible for us to do.

Think for a moment about how many things, though, are possible for you. Now pursue that thought a little further and think about how many things you are capable of doing that you should not do. That list is pretty long, too! That means that Satan has an almost unlimited number of options when he decides to run *temptation with the possible* against you.

Because of these myriad options, Satan can pick and choose which one he wants to tempt you with. Early on, you will be far more tempted to do the things that are easy. If you really want to get a good grade on a test, but you also know that you did not study as much as you should have, the temptation to sneak a peek at the answer sheet of the student beside or in front of you will be strong—much stronger than the desire to steal the answer key from the teacher, for instance. Stealing the answer key (and subsequently returning it undetected) would require much more planning, skill, and stealth. On the other hand, peeking at another student's answer sheet involves little effort (or risk) but could be very rewarding. Little time is needed, little planning is required, and there is little risk of being caught (since cheating is often difficult to prove). Satan knows all of this, and that is why he would push this option much harder than the possibility of stealing the answer key.

After a few times of cheating off another student's paper, however, you would probably get pretty comfortable doing it. You would find all kinds of ways to justify it in your own mind. "I thought that was the answer, I just wanted to make sure," you might tell yourself. You would get so comfortable that you might stop thinking about the fact that you are doing something wrong. You may decide you could probably get away with trying something more risky, yet more certain—writing answers on your hand or an index card before class and peeking during the test. The more comfortable you get with cheating, the more likely you are to continue, upping the ante in the process. Soon, stealing the answer key from the teacher, or ordering an answer key from the publisher doesn't seem like such a big deal. And, you're guaranteed to get the right answers as long as you're not caught. Good grades, guaranteed!

How slippery a slope this is! How easy it is to progress from peeking at another student's paper to making cheating a regular part of our lives! And if we get comfortable cheating on tests, why not cheat on homework, athletic contests, or board games? And, (eventually) our taxes? If we can cheat in all those places and get away with it, why not cheat our employers? Many workers do enough work to get by (and make a good impression for the boss) but they sit back and take it easy when no one is looking. Just running the *temptation with the possible* play successfully one time can completely shut down your defenses and make it possible for Satan to keep running it over and over again. Before you know it, he is scoring time after time and really running up the score. You find yourself looking at the scoreboard and asking yourself "How did he score all those points? Where is my defense?" Unlike football, where the defense tends to learn from its mistakes, we believers are *more* likely to be beaten a second time by the same play, and our chance of failure goes up if we don't even recognize that we're yielding to temptation and committing sin.

The *temptation with the possible* play exploits the things that are possible for us to do, and those that are easy for us to do. How tempted are you to rob a bank? Not very, because the odds of success are slim. However, you might be tempted to steal a candy bar or a pack of gum from the local convenience store, because it does not require much effort and the likelihood of getting caught is much smaller. Does that make it any less wrong? That candy bar might be just the first step down that slippery slope. No one who has ever robbed a bank started by robbing a bank. Sin starts small and builds, gradually getting bigger and bigger.

Take lying, for instance. There are numerous times every day when we can lie, and lying usually comes fairly easily, even naturally. Our sin nature has a strong instinct for self-defense and self- preservation, and acknowledging weakness or error is not a part of that make up. So, we sometimes lie, or stretch the truth, or tell only a partial truth, because we don't want to deal with the unpleasantness of telling the whole truth.

It started way back in the book of Genesis. When Cain killed his brother Abel, he knew he had done something wrong. Then God confronted him about it and asked him where Abel was. How did Cain respond? By lying! He didn't hesitate. He was asked, and his immediate, sin-nature response was to lie. Now to you and me it probably seems foolish; after all, how can you expect to get away with lying to God Himself? You are probably thinking, "Not too bright, Cain. I might lie from time to time, but I sure would not be stupid enough to lie to God!" But hang on just a second—are you sure about that? When we lie—regardless of to whom we are actually speaking—are we not lying to God? God knows about our lies. He already knows the truth, just as He did when He asked Cain where Abel was. When we lie to friends, to parents, to teachers, to a boyfriend or girlfriend, to anyone at all, we are lying in the presence of God.

Unfortunately, in this matter of resisting temptation, there are some things that are far easier for us to do today than they were for our parents or grandparents. Smoking is easy today. I doubt there is a teen in the United States that couldn't get his hands on cigarettes pretty quickly if the motivation was strong enough. The good news, though, is that cigarette use among teenagers has been declining for a long time. The message that tobacco use can kill, or result in serious health problems, seems to be getting through.

Pornography, however, is a growing problem, and a grave one. Years ago it was very difficult for a young person to see pornography. There was none of it in the movies, or on television. Even married couples on TV shows sometimes slept in different beds! Suggestive posters and "girlie" magazines were kept hidden away. Gradually, however, the movies began to allow more and more explicit sexual content and now partial nudity is not at all uncommon in a Hollywood film, or even on a television show. Grocery stores, drug stores, convenience stores, and bookstores all carry magazines with explicit sexual content right on the cover. A magazine with a naked woman on the front—hands strategically placed—is no longer a rarity. A few years ago I received a copy of *The Sporting News* in the mail with a naked woman on the cover, lying in a bunch of baseballs! I subscribed to the magazine because I like baseball, and I like to keep up on the scouting reports, the trades, and other bits of baseball news, yet it came to me, delivered right to my mailbox, with a picture on the cover that I would be embarrassed for my daughter to see, and that I would never allow the boys I worked with to see.

Pornography is, of course, readily available on the Internet today. Young people can see hard-core pornography in less than thirty seconds from almost anywhere in the country with just a few key strokes and a click of the mouse. The average age of exposure to pornography today is under ten, and kids between twelve and seventeen make up the largest consumers of Internet pornography in the United States! Satan knows what he is doing.

Girls, this danger applies to you as well as to guys. Females are just as much into Internet pornography as males are and females are, in fact, much more likely to engage in Internet chat about sexual topics according to a number of studies. Magazines targeted at teenage girls spend the bulk of their pages explaining what pants will best show off one's posterior, which make up and clothing styles will get the most attention from guys, and what sex tips teenage daters "need" to know. All of this reflects a culture that is completely saturated with sex. It is no surprise, then, that sexual temptation—and specifically the availability of porn—is one of Satan's biggest assets when running *temptation with the possible.*

Another vice that is far more accessible for young people today than it was a generation or two ago is drug use. Sure, if you look at the statistics you will likely see that marijuana use has declined, and that the use of crack cocaine has declined. But that doesn't mean that the abuse of drugs—legal and illegal drugs—has truly declined. For example, there are more young people today than ever before using steroids in an effort to get bigger and stronger, to gain an advantage over their opponents on the court, on the field, or on the mat. There is more methamphetamine use today than ever before.

Inhalant abuse is growing, too. Talk about easy access! Inhalants can be found almost anywhere, in any home, school, or workplace. Products that have been designed and marketed to help with such tasks as stain removal, paint removal, air freshening, and cleaning are being used to get high. The most frightening thing about inhalants is that its users can die the very first time they inhale. Some people die the first time, some die the fiftieth, and others don't die even after five hundred uses. Some survive but in a vegetative state; I have heard of young people—teens—now living in nursing homes because inhalant abuse destroyed their brain and their ability to control their bodily functions.

And what about the rampant abuse of prescription drugs? Psychotropic drugs and pain killers are very popular among teens who don't need them and haven't had them prescribed. There is a market in schools—in every community—for ADHD medication and prescription pain relievers. Some teens are actually happy when a friend has his wisdom teeth extracted or a parent has back surgery, because they know it will give them an opportunity to get their hands on some strong medication! And valuable medication, too; some prescription drugs can bring three to seven dollars per pill. Over-the-counter drugs are also being abused: Cold medicines and allergy medications in particular are popular. When mixed and chased with alcohol these drugs become extremely dangerous. In an effort to find new and more effective ways to get high teens are experimenting with their lives. They're playing Russian roulette, pulling the trigger with new combinations of drugs and alcohol.

All of these things are possible for you to do, and many of them are also easy. The choice is yours, because the fact is that no one can stop you from engaging in these behaviors. Your school and your parents may have rules and consequences in place that will make it more difficult for you to do these things, but in the end, you are not a puppet. No one can control your every action; it comes down to your own choices. You'll be faced with these temptations on a regular basis. Don't think that it will get easier as you get older or that these temptations are going to disappear, because that's not going to happen. Satan is forever learning, forever getting better, smarter and more creative, and he will keep running this play against you for the rest of your life. Now that you know the play, however, you can be on the watch for it, and be prepared to defend against it.

Instant Replay

Satan tempted Jesus after He had been fasting for more than a month. He appealed to Jesus' most basic desire at that moment—food. Turning the stones into bread would have been possible for Jesus to do, but it would have been wrong.

Satan tempts you the same way. He tempts you with something that appeals to you, that may even seem to offer a solution to a need that you have. Whatever it is, it will be something that is possible for you to do, and it will probably be fairly easy to do as well. But that doesn't make it right. If the action you're being confronted with will result in doing something wrong, then you are facing *temptation with the possible.* Look for it, keep your defenses up, and stop letting Satan beat you with that play!

Chapter 2

Play #2: Temptation to Prove

The second play in Satan's playbook is the *temptation to prove*. This play tries to lure you into letting your defenses down by fakery: You go after the guy you think has the ball, while the ball is really being taken downfield for a touchdown by someone you didn't even notice. With this play, Satan encourages doubt in you and tempts you to disprove those doubts.

If the quarterback is successful in getting you to follow his fake, your entire defense will end up chasing a player who doesn't have the ball. Similarly, when Satan is successful in planting doubts, you can miss what he is really trying to do. You can be so wrapped up in proving something that isn't even important that you can get involved in sin before you know it.

Satan ran this play twice against Christ in the wilderness, but it's interesting to note that in order to maximize his chances of success he always used it in conjunction with another option. As we saw in chapter one, Satan said to Christ (in Matthew 4:3), "If you are the Son of God, just turn those stones into bread." In other words, "If You really are who You say You are, prove it."

Satan knew, of course, that Jesus was the Son of God, and Jesus was well aware of the fact that Satan knew who He was. After all, Jesus had known Satan (as Lucifer) before he was cast out of heaven. Jesus was there when Satan was created! However, Satan was hoping to get Jesus flustered so that He would, in the heat of the moment, turn the stones into bread just to shut Satan up. If Jesus had used His divine power purely to disprove Satan's questioning and to satisfy His own wants, it would have been a misuse of that power, and it would have been sin. That, of course, was Satan's goal—to get Jesus to sin. If Jesus had sinned, He would no longer have been able to fulfill God's plan, because He would no longer have been the sinless sacrifice that God required.

This play didn't work the first time Satan ran it, even when combined with the *temptation with the possible*, so he ran the play again in verse 6 when he took Jesus up to the pinnacle of the temple and said to Him, "If you really are the Son of God why not just jump off of here? You know God will send angels to catch you, and nothing will happen. Go ahead...jump. Prove that You really are who You say You are." Once again, though, it would have been a misuse of Jesus' power as God to jump off the temple simply to cause angels to come and catch Him. It would have been sin.

Satan runs this same play against us. He doesn't tempt us to prove that we can turn stones into bread or jump off of high places, but he tempts us to prove other things—things like friendship, love, courage, or the ability to fit in.

From a very early age children are tempted to prove their friendship. Children who aren't even out of kindergarten can be heard saying, "Then I won't be your friend anymore" or "I'll be your friend if you [fill in the blank]." All this, of course, is a means of manipulation. It's a way of using power to force others to do something for us. Hard to believe that four- and five-year-olds can use power to influence the behavior of others, isn't it? But you did the same thing! When your friend, or even another child who was not your friend, didn't want to cooperate with you, didn't you whip out the "prove you're worthy of my friendship" weapon that every little kid carries around in his back pocket?

Naturally, Satan uses the same approach with us. Sometimes—intentionally or not—friends are actually working as Satan's agents when they use this strategy against us. Every human being has been tempted to do something that he or she would otherwise never have done, simply because he (or she) thought it would impress someone or secure a friendship. And it doesn't just happen with little kids; it happens with tweens, teens, and adults, and it takes on many different forms. Consider these approaches:

- "If you were really a team player…"
- "It's in the best interest of the company…"
- "If you really cared about this family…"

Sound familiar? Any relationship, no matter how wonderful and enjoyable, can be instantly converted into a means of extortion or manipulation.

Of course, the boyfriend-girlfriend relationship, more than any other kind, is subject to this kind of manipulation. Many teens today pressure their boyfriend or girlfriend into sexual behavior by saying, "If you really loved me you'd do this." This statement, sadly, is a complete reversal of the truth. In reality, if two teenagers loved each other the way God created love, they would never pressure one another into doing something wrong. Love, as God intended it, always puts the other person first; it always wants what is best for the other person.

When Satan runs the *temptation to prove* play against us, his goal is to get us to question what we believe to be true—even what we *know* to be true. Jesus Christ knew that He was the Son of God. Satan hoped that he could either get Christ to doubt His divinity, or that He would test His powers to prove to Himself that it was true. With us, if enough doubt is planted, we start to wonder; we start to ask ourselves, "Is that really true? Am I really who I think I am? Do I really believe what I think I believe?"

And if this approach doesn't work, Satan has a back-up plan. If he can't get us to doubt what we know about ourselves, he'll try to get others to express doubts about us, hoping that we will yield to temptation in an effort to prove the doubting person wrong. Satan was well aware that Christ was the Son of God, but he hoped that by expressing doubt and skepticism he could get Jesus to prove who He really was. This tactic works by preying on our pride. No one likes to be questioned, and most of us are too proud to ignore the rumors, conjectures or doubts that others express about us from time to time.

The difficult thing about this particular temptation is that sometimes it is necessary to prove something by our actions. It is not enough to just "talk the talk"—sometimes we have to "walk the walk." The Bible makes it plain that our faith in Christ is to be acted out—that is, it should be demonstrated in what we do and how we live. In 1 John 3:18 we read that it's not enough to love in word or tongue, we must also love in deed and in truth.

James, too, talks about showing faith by works, and even states that faith without works is dead. James 2:15-16 challenges the person who thinks that encouragement or a kind word is evidence of faith. James gives a very poignant and pointed example: If we see another person naked and hungry—situations we can easily imagine, even if we've never experienced them—what good is it to tell that person, "think warm thoughts and imagine eating a full meal"? What good would it do to say, "I hope that you can find a blanket and get something to eat"? And when it comes right down to it, what point is there in only saying, "I will pray for you"?

The only true way to show love to him is to give him some blankets, some clothing, or something to eat. Knowing the right thing to say—the politically correct thing, or even the religiously-expected thing—is not worth anything unless we back it up with action. Words never warmed anyone who was cold or fed anyone who was hungry.

The most effective temptation is the one that looks and sounds as if it could be true. Satan knows that he's an expert at creating the appearance of truth. To give a modern parallel, some companies make a lot of money by designing and selling products that look almost exactly like designer, name-brand merchandise, but they leave off the logo or alter some minor detail. People then buy what looks like a high-dollar, fashionable item at a much lower price than the genuine article. These cheaper imitations are called "knockoffs."

There are certain brands of clothing now that are in style, and you want very much to wear those trendy items to help you to fit in. You're also aware that wearing a knockoff is often worse than wearing something that is not in style. You would be better off, in other words, to wear a paisley shirt to school than to wear an imitation Aeropostale or American Eagle shirt. It seems as if it is more acceptable to be ignorant of style than to be aware of it and not be able to afford it.

I still remember being caught in that situation in middle school. Nike shoes were quite popular then, as they are now. I had never owned a pair of Nike shoes, and my parents were not about to buy me a pair simply for the name, so I got a pair of shoes that were the department store's own brand. They looked exactly like Nike shoes—the colors were the same and the design was the same—but they didn't have the Nike "swoosh." I was pleased with my new shoes until one afternoon, in gym class, another boy commented on my "imitation Nikes." I can still remember that boy's name, because that remark stung me; it hurt. I was trying to fit in, and I'd been busted. My look-alikes were not going to cut it, and he made sure that I knew it. The absence of the logo was an announcement that I didn't have real Nikes.

In the same way, Satan tempts us with something that looks like the real deal. It looks like the truth. But if we know what we're looking for—if we know what the logo or label of the truth looks like—we'll be able to spot the imitation easily. You may have heard the famous illustration (a favorite with pastors) about the United States Secret Service and counterfeit money. Although the Secret Service is best known for protecting the president and other important political leaders, it is also responsible for tracking down counterfeiters. The agents that work in the counterfeit units don't study counterfeit money. Instead, they study genuine, legal bills until they know every detail. They become so familiar with the real money—with the truth—that they can easily spot the imitation. That's what God wants of us—to study His truth and know it so well that we will easily be able to spot a fake.

The passages we've looked at indicate that our actions should demonstrate, or prove, our faith. If we see someone naked and hungry, and we have the ability to meet those needs, our actions should prove our faith—we should provide food and clothing. Scripture tells us that we are to love one another, and to love our neighbor as ourselves. How we treat other people; how we speak to them; how we help someone who has dropped their books or has a flat tire; how we stick up for the nerd that everyone else makes fun of—these actions prove that we are Christians. Our walk should back up our talk.

Satan, though, takes that biblical truth, and twists it for his own benefit. He tries to convince us that we have to prove our love for our friends by lying for them or helping them cheat on a test. He tries to tell girls that they have to prove their love for their boyfriends by having sex. He tells boys that they have to prove that they belong in the group by breaking into someone's home and stealing, or by beating up someone. All of these things are false, but unless we know the truth, we may fall for the lies.

A sad truth is that many young people have never experienced true love. Many teens have not grown up with a mom and dad, or other caregivers, who loved them unconditionally. Because of that, they are yearning for someone who will love them, accept them, and care about them. This may describe you or one of your friends right now. If so, you need to know the truth about the love of God.

Do you know that God loves you unconditionally? There is nothing that you can do to earn His love. Regardless of how hard you try, how much money you earn, how famous or successful you become, none of that will earn you love. It may not even make you happy! It can enable you to have a lot of fun, but it will never fill the longing that you have for unconditional acceptance. God did not design humans to treat each other the way we so often do; the hurt and rejection that we cause one another is a byproduct of sin, and it hurts God to see it. And because He does love us unconditionally, He has provided a way for us to know His love—through Jesus Christ.

It's great to have goals and accomplishments in life, and it's admirable to work hard to achieve a goal, but there is nothing you can do to earn God's love.

Instant Replay

Satan tempted Jesus to prove that He was the Son of God. Likewise, Satan tempts you to prove things—perhaps that you're popular (and part of the "in crowd"); or that you love someone; or that you're not scared.

When you find yourself tempted to prove something, ask yourself if what you are being tempted to do is something that you *should* (not *could*) do. People who really love you will never tempt you to do anything that you shouldn't, and they will never ask you to do anything in order to prove yourself to them.

Chapter 3

Play #3: Temptation with Protection

In verse 5 of Matthew 4 Satan takes Jesus up to the pinnacle of the temple in Jerusalem. The pinnacle of the temple was probably located on the corner that overlooked the Kidron Valley. From the tip of the pinnacle to the bottom of the valley would have been about 450 feet—or the equivalent of a 45 story building! Satan and Jesus Christ are atop this great height and Satan says to Jesus, "Why don't you just jump off? The Scriptures say that God will send angels to catch You, and nothing will happen. Go for it!"

At first glance, this could be seen as another example of the *temptation to prove.* Satan is saying, "If you really are the Son of God, just jump. If You are who You say You are, God will make sure nothing happens to You, so prove it to me." Never underestimate Satan's willingness to run the same play twice in a row. Sometimes, in fact, we are more vulnerable to a particular play when we just successfully defended against it, because we usually don't expect to see it again so quickly. It's important to be ready for anything that Satan may throw at us.

We also see in this passage, though, the next play in Satan's play book—*temptation with protection*. Satan tempts Jesus to jump off of the pinnacle by assuring Him that no harm will come to Him. You can almost see Satan whispering to Jesus "You won't get hurt, I promise. And just imagine how much fun it will be…the thrill of the jump and the free fall all the way down…and then the soft landing in the arms of angels. It will be such a rush! Go for it!"

Satan tempts us in the same way. He entices us to engage in sinful behavior by telling us that we won't get caught, and then he tries to sweeten the deal by offering protection—telling us that we won't get hurt—and we fall for it all the time! We talk ourselves into thinking that it's not really that big a deal.

Most people aren't tempted to do something that they *know* will result in physical or emotional pain, but they're willing to engage in risky behavior if there's just a chance of risk. They fall for Satan's line when he says, "That won't happen to you." It's the difference between *might* and *know*—the possible versus the definite.

For example, a few years ago my family was staying at my brother's house to celebrate Thanksgiving. My brother had e-mailed me weeks before to say that he wanted to play football on Thanksgiving morning, and that he was lining up players for the big game. Growing up, my father, brother and I loved to play football. We were involved in scores of neighborhood and family football games, so it was not uncommon for us to play on Thanksgiving Day. My brother's plan sounded like a great idea, and I was looking forward to the game.

The day before Thanksgiving was a dreary day, and it rained all day long. We discussed several times whether or not we would try to play the next day. Thanksgiving morning, though, was mostly clear, with just occasional drizzle. We decided to play. We ate breakfast, got dressed, and headed over to a local high school for the big game. Now, as I was brushing my teeth that morning, I was thinking about the possibility of someone getting hurt, and how an injury could ruin the holiday for the family. But that thought faded as my brother told me how excited he was about playing together—something we hadn't done for a long time.

It was cold, and the field was wet and slippery. I had forgotten to bring cleats, so I had to play in my athletic shoes. We jogged around a little, tossed the ball a few times, set up some cones, and divided into teams. We were ready to start the big game! The other team kicked off to us, and my team started on our "20 yard line." My dad (our quarterback) huddled us up and called the play. My brother and I lined up together on the right; he would run a slant across the field, and I was to start slow and then go long.

The center snapped the ball, and my brother streaked across the field. I took a few slow steps and then took off down field. I burned past the defender, and suddenly I was wide open. My dad threw the ball toward me, but his pass was short, and when I tried to go back to the ball my feet slipped out from under me. I fell hard to the ground, hitting my hip first and then my shoulder. Severe pain shot through my shoulder and my arm, and immediately I knew that I was really hurt. I had never felt such pain before.

Someone helped me up; I felt dizzy and sick. Everyone told me later that I was as white as a sheet and that my arm and hand were in very unnatural positions. Just like that, on the very first play, I was done. I was out of the game, and it looked as though I'd be spending the day in the emergency room, eating crackers and Jell-O, rather than enjoying turkey and my mom's twice-baked potatoes.

Fortunately that didn't happen, and the day was not ruined, but my arm was indeed injured and it took over a week for the pain to subside. But the point is, if I had *known* that Thanksgiving morning that I was going to be hurt, I wouldn't have played in the game, no matter how much my brother wanted me to play. I played knowing that I *might* get hurt, but I convinced myself that it wasn't going to happen. I had never been seriously injured in any athletic event, and I had spent most of my life playing sports. *I didn't think it would happen to me.*

This is exactly how we tend to respond when Satan runs *temptation with protection* against us. We allow ourselves to be swayed, against our better judgment, by the promise of protection and the belief that "it won't happen to me."

The consequences of sin don't always hit people the first time. Now, sometimes a guy will die the first time he abuses inhalants or a girl will get pregnant the first time she engages in sexual activity. Sometimes kids will get caught the very first time they steal something. Usually, though, there are no consequences that first time, and that means people are far more likely to do "it" again—whatever "it" is.

Getting away with sin is a lot like gambling: Win often enough, and you tend to keep playing. The second time it's a lot easier to give into the temptation, and the third time is even easier. When someone gets high and gets away with it, he will probably get high again, and the same applies to other sins.

It all goes back to the difference between *might* and *will,* or *know.*

How many times have you heard someone say, "If I had only known…."? The reality is, no one has ever been tempted by the truth. If every package of cigarettes boldly proclaimed, "WARNING: USE OF THIS PRODUCT WILL CERTAINLY RESULT IN A SLOW, PAINFUL

DEATH FROM CANCER," it's unlikely that many people would smoke. The package doesn't say that, though, because cigarettes don't *always* cause cancer. If someone *knew* before cheating that he would certainly be caught, he wouldn't cheat. If he *knew* he would contract AIDS before having sex, he would probably abstain. If she *knew* she would die if she tried to drive home after having a few drinks, she probably wouldn't drive. But because the result is not certain, people let themselves believe that it won't happen. People believe they will be protected.

In order to understand *temptation with protection* it's important to understand Satan's goals. He would actually prefer that you experience some short-term protection, because that makes you all the more likely to engage in that sinful behavior again and again—and again. And the more you do it, the more you enjoy it, and the deeper you get into it, the more likely you are to get other people involved in doing it with you. But Satan has no long-term interest in your protection; Satan isn't interested in protecting you for your own sake, because (of course) he doesn't care about you.

Satan wasn't interested in protecting Jesus Christ that day on the pinnacle of the temple. Satan knew who Jesus was, and he knew that the angels would not allow Jesus to plunge to His death at the bottom of the Kidron Valley. His motive was to ruin Jesus. Jesus would not have died, even if He had jumped, but He would have sinned by testing God and by abusing His power as the Son of God. And if He had sinned, Jesus would no longer have qualified as the perfect sacrifice, and God's plan of redemption would have been ruined. *That* was Satan's motive and plan. Satan's plans always lead to destruction.

Similarly, Satan wants to get you so wrapped up in sin that you have no interest in God or salvation. After all, if you die without Christ then you will go to hell, and then Satan will have you forever. Satan is also interested in destroying a believer's reputation and testimony for Christ. If you become engrossed in sin, he might be interested in your short-term protection so that everyone around you will be sickened by your hypocrisy. In the end, though, he wants you dead before you have a chance to repent and get right with God and lead souls to Christ. Remember, once you are saved, Satan has lost you, and he can never get you back. He just wants to see your testimony destroyed, and then he wants you to leave earth as quickly as possible. Satan's offer of protection is simply one more lie in his plan to lead you into the trap of sin.

Instant Replay

Satan tempted Jesus to jump off the temple by reminding Him that He would be protected. Although Satan was technically right in this instance—Jesus would have been physically protected—the damage would still have been done. By misusing His powers as God, Jesus would have sinned.

When you sin, there will seldom be immediate physical consequences, but the non-physical damage may be severe. Destroyed relationships, damaged reputations, and emotional scarring can last far longer than broken bones or physical illness. And, of course, there is the damage to your relationship with Christ and your ability to be a testimony for Him.

Still, physical consequences, like sexually transmitted diseases, brain damage, pregnancy, chemical addiction, and even death can result from your choice to sin. In the end, no matter what lies Satan may tell you, there is no protection against the consequences of sin.

Chapter 4

Play #4: Temptation with Perversion

The dictionary says that to pervert something means to "cause to turn away from what is good or true; to twist the meaning or sense of." Satan likes to run his perversion attack on the truth of God's Word. Everything that the Scripture contains is good and true, but Satan is a master at twisting the meaning of what God has said and using his twisted version to entice us to sin. What God intended for our pleasure and our good is perverted by Satan and presented in a way that is opposed to what God intended.

In verse 6 we see a change in Satan's approach: he shifts from tempting Jesus to prove that He *is* the Son of God to tempting Jesus *because* He is the Son of God. The protection that Satan offers to Jesus in this passage comes from Psalm 91:11-12: "For he will command his angels concerning you to guard you in all your ways. On their hands they will bear you up, lest you strike your foot against a stone." Satan twists the meaning of the passage, though, to tempt Jesus to sin. Satan knows Scripture! In fact, he knows it far better than you or I do, or than the world's most brilliant theologian. First of all, Satan has lived through and personally observed everything that the Bible talks about. Second, Satan has the ability to speak directly to God (see the beginning of the story of Job). Third, Satan has memorized the Scriptures specifically so that he can use God's Word against us. The most effective lies in the world are those that contain an element of truth, and unless we know the truth, we become prime targets for Satan's perversion. Unfortunately, many Christians today—adults as well as young people—don't take the time or exert the effort to truly study the Word of God. The result is that many of us are still "babes in Christ," meaning that we know enough about the Bible to talk the talk, but not enough to see through the lies that Satan throws at us.

Here's an example of a truly ridiculous modern-day perversion: Some maintain that since God created marijuana, it must be good for us. After all, God wouldn't create something that wasn't beneficial—right? There are numerous problems with this position. First of all, it ignores the reality of the Fall. Many things changed after Adam and Eve sinned. They were banished from the Garden of Eden; physical death became a reality; child birth was permanently associated with physical pain; and physical labor—"the sweat of your face"—would now be required to grow and obtain food, because thorns, thistles and weeds grow on the earth.

Second, it may well be true that God created marijuana. It is foolish, however, to reason that since God created it, and since smoking it creates a physical sensation that some people find pleasurable, it must therefore be *okay* with God for us to use marijuana. There are many things that God created that are fine or harmless in and of themselves but that can be easily abused. That's all part of the free will that God gave to us as human beings. God gave us the ability to think, to reason, and to make our own choices. He did not create legions of robots to operate exactly as He programmed them.

Just because I *can* smoke marijuana doesn't mean that I *should*. You can't find "marijuana" in your Bible anywhere, regardless of the translation you use. (Even though there are some creative and contemporary translations out there!) However, that doesn't mean that the Bible has nothing to say about the subject, because it does. The Bible makes it very clear that we are not to be under the influence of any substance. If I smoke marijuana, or consume too much alcohol, I can't be fully in control of myself. Anytime that I'm not fully in control of my body—completely able to perceive my surroundings, rationally process the events and choices before me and then make a decision logically—I am necessarily under the control of something else. I am *under the influence.*

Scripture also makes it clear that the body of the believer is the dwelling place of the Holy Spirit—a temple, and that we are to present ourselves "holy and acceptable to God" (Romans 12:1). This can't be done when we are under the influence of drugs or alcohol. *To be holy* literally means to be separate; we are to be separated from the filth of this world by clinging to God.

Another perversion that Satan uses is that since God created sex, and since God gave each human being a sex drive, then it is okay to have sex, since it is fulfilling a God-given desire. Not true! God did create sex and He did give each of us a sex drive, and sex is a beautiful thing—as God created it. But He did not create humans to have numerous sexual relationships. He did not create humans to engage in sex solely for the physical pleasure involved. Sex is much more than a physical act; it's a tremendously emotional experience, as well. God has made it clear that sex within marriage is appropriate, but that sex outside of marriage—that includes both premarital and extramarital sex—is wrong. There are numerous passages of Scripture which address this exact issue. (If you're interested in reading them for yourself, take a look at the reference list at the back of this book).

Another of Satan's perversions is the lie that the biblical prohibition against sex before or outside of marriage only pertains to sexual intercourse. In fact, many so-called experts in the field, and plenty of trendy youth publications, will tell you that other kinds of sexual activity are perfectly acceptable, a normal part of growing up, and not technically "having sex." Sexual experimentation is considered to be almost a required part of the teen years. Let's be blunt: sexual activity between unmarried persons, including _______ sex (regardless of what word you put in the blank or what kind of sex it is), outercourse (having sex with your clothes on),or any other physical act between two individuals involving the male and female sex organs, is wrong and a sin against God. Do not be fooled by Satan's perversion of what God intended to be a wonderful thing between husband and wife.

There is an overwhelming emphasis in our culture on safe sex. We are told that it's fine to experiment sexually as long as we make sure that condoms are used and that every precaution is taken to avoid the possibility of getting (or giving) a sexually transmitted disease. The late Adrian Rogers had an excellent response to this "safe-sex" mantra—sex, *as God designed it*, was never meant to be dangerous! In other words, if you practice sex the way God intended it, it *will* be safe—the first time, and every time. It's really a lot like those products that come with ridiculous warning labels, simply because someone once used the product the wrong way and got hurt.

In reality, common sense should tell us that if God designed sex and we practice it the way He designed it, we'll be safe. Many companies make products that come with a warranty—a written guarantee that the product will do what it was designed to do for a certain period of time, and that if it fails during that period, the company will repair or replace it. But almost every warranty also includes some sort of clause that negates the warranty if the purchaser uses the product in a manner other than that for which it was intended. If I buy a new chain saw and it fails to cut the limbs of a tree in my back yard, the company will probably replace it for me, because the saw doesn't do what it was designed to do. But if I break the chain saw trying to cut through my concrete patio, the company is off the hook—because I broke the chain saw trying to use it in a way that was it never intended to be used.

Similarly, God has given us a warranty of sorts. If we engage in sex the way He designed it, we won't have to worry about STDs. But if we start to engage in sex in other ways, we void the warranty, and it's not God's fault that there are very real and dangerous consequences. And just as it would be no one's fault but my own if I broke my chain saw trying to cut through concrete, it is really no one's fault but my own if I contract an STD as a result of having sex with someone I should not be having sex with.

Further, sex was designed by God to be enjoyed between a husband and a wife, meaning a man and a woman. This brings us to another perversion of God's Word—one that has been enjoying widespread acceptance. It's the idea that God created some people to be homosexual. They cannot help it, Satan says, and it is perfectly natural for some individuals to be interested in members of their own sex. Now, God did create homosexuals—He created every person who has ever lived—but He did not create them *as* homosexuals or *to be* homosexuals. All homosexual tendencies are a result of sin. (For specific Scriptures addressing this issue, see the reference list in the back of the book. Several verses state explicitly that sexual activity between a man and a man, or a woman and a woman, is wrong and is considered by God to be an abomination). God would not—indeed, as a holy God He cannot—create humans who are programmed to engage in behavior that He says is wrong.

However, take care that you're not fooled by another perversion closely related to this one: the idea that God hates homosexuals. God doesn't hate homosexuals, and no Christian has a right to hate them, either. He created them, He loves them, and He wants to have a relationship with them. He stands ready to forgive their sin, welcome them into His family, and give them the gift of eternal life. If you have homosexual tendencies or interests, God did not create you that way, but He still loves you, and He is able to help you overcome those desires. If you know someone who is interested in the gay lifestyle, or is openly practicing homosexuality, God loves that person and He expects you to do the same.

Part of the cultural war around us is the constant drawing of battle lines. When we take sides, we should be concerned with one thing and one thing only—what side is God on? We don't need to worry whether or not God is on our side; our only concern should be whether or not we are on *God's* side. God loves the sinner, but hates the sin. We should do likewise.

Much of this chapter is about sex for the simple reason that there are so many perversions of sex facing you every day. As a teen, you'll hear tens of thousands of perversions of God's truth before you ever reach adulthood. Evolution is a perversion. The notion that you have to look a certain way, be a certain size or race or ___________ (you fill the blank) to be accepted or loved is a perversion. Yet half of all the perversions that you're exposed to each day are either directly or indirectly about sex. There are dozens of magazines marketed to teens that regularly provide sex advice, but sadly, very few (if any) provide readers with the truth about sex as God intended it.

Another very common satanic perversion relates to personal wealth or prosperity. There are scores of Christian leaders and teachers who regularly state that God intends for His followers to have material wealth. If you truly love God and are following His will for your life, they teach, then you will be healthy and wealthy! This so-called prosperity gospel is a perversion of God's Word. There is no biblical support for the position that God wants all His followers to be rich. Although some believers in the Bible were notably wealthy—Abraham and Job come to mind, among others—there is no biblical support for the position that God *will* bless His followers with material prosperity. Jesus Christ Himself was not rich while He was on earth, and neither were His disciples. Paul was not wealthy. Very few of the early believers in the Bible had money. Why would the Bible teach that those who follow Christ's teachings will have something that neither He nor His personal disciples had? It doesn't make any sense logically, or theologically, either. If you study the Bible, you will see that the Scriptures don't support the idea that all believers will be rich. When you hear someone preaching this way, beware of the *temptation with perversion.*

In fact, we should always be aware of anything that we hear proclaimed by man as God's truth. Paul himself told the early believers that they should look into the Scriptures and see for themselves whether what Paul taught was consistent with what Jesus had said. That is good advice for us, too! Many people assume that if a preacher says it, it must be true—especially if the preacher is on television; there seems to be a common belief that if the pastor's ministry is successful enough for him to have a television program, anything he says must be true. Nothing could be further from the truth! Some of the worst Bible teaching is broadcast over our nation's airwaves. We must be very careful to compare what we hear with what the Bible says.

For example, the pastor of the largest church in the United States has stated publicly and boldly that he never talks about sin in his church. Anyone who has ever studied the Bible knows that it talks about sin plenty. Only by understanding sin can we understand our sinfulness, and only by understanding our sinfulness can we understand our need for salvation. Romans 3:23 makes it clear: "All have sinned and fall short of the glory of God." How can we know that we have fallen short if no one tells us we've sinned? Romans 6:23 states that, "The wages of sin is death, but the free gift of God is eternal life in Christ Jesus our Lord." If we don't know we've earned hell, we will never know that we need salvation. Anyone who claims to be a minister of the gospel of Christ but refuses to talk about sin is preaching a perverted gospel. It is just this sort of syrupy, feel-good theology that has thousands of people today focused more on how to feel good about themselves then on how to obey Christ. Sadly, *temptation with perversion* is still a very effective part of Satan's playbook.

Instant Replay

To pervert something means to twist its meaning, and Satan loves to pervert the truth of the Bible. Some of his favorite things to pervert are God's design for sex, the Bible's teachings about material and financial blessing, and the reality of sin. The only way to know for sure if something is true or perverted is to compare it to the Bible. Diligently study the Scriptures, and check and double-check everything you hear. Only ideas that line up with Scripture are true.

Chapter 5

Play #5: Temptation with a Peek

After Satan's first attempts at tempting Christ failed—temptation with the possible, temptation to prove, temptation with protection, and temptation with perversion—he turned to another that has always worked well for him from the beginning: *temptation with a peek*. Any good football coach keeps trying to find a way to breach the defense and win the game. In the game we're talking about here, a victory for Satan means getting us to sin. So, when we successfully defend against one temptation, he continues to try others, always looking for a weakness in our defense.

Temptation with a peek is an incredibly effective play in Satan's playbook. In Matthew 5:8, Satan led Jesus up to "an exceedingly high mountain, and showed Him all the kingdoms of the world and their glory." I love the mountains, and a few years ago my wife and I went to look at some mountain-top property that we were considering purchasing. The view was one of the most spectacular things I have ever seen. We could literally see, on that clear morning, a place fifty miles away! It was incredible. But I can't imagine a mountain so high that you could see all the kingdoms of the world. Whether Matthew is using hyperbole here or not doesn't really matter; Satan took Jesus up to the top of a very high mountain, and this vantage point gave them an incredible view of the world below.

Satan's goal was to show Jesus what He could have if He would only yield—that is, bow down and worship Satan. Interestingly, Jesus did not rebuke Satan by telling him that the kingdoms of the world were not his to give. This is strong evidence for the power that Satan has as the prince of this earth. It would have done Satan no good to offer Jesus something he could not give him, nor would Jesus have had any reason to entertain Satan's offer.

Let me put it another way. It would not be effective for me to offer you $1 million to bow down and declare me the most extraordinary human being God ever created because (a) I could not pay you $1 million, and (b) you would know that I couldn't pay you $1 million. Therefore, you wouldn't be tempted in the least, because you would know that my offer was hollow. However, if I opened a briefcase in front of you that was filled with hundred-dollar bills, you *would* be tempted, because you had a *peek*, and you had seen enough to know that I might have $1 million. You would give the temptation considerably more thought because you had seen that I could deliver on my offer. You would probably be particularly tempted if we were in some remote corner of the world with no one else around.

In the case of Satan's temptation of Christ, it is safe to assume that there was no one else present, so we can also safely assume that Jesus could have bowed down to Satan without another person on earth knowing about it. God, however, would have known. Jesus would have broken

God's commandment that we worship no other God, and He would have denied Himself and His Father. Further, as stated earlier, if Jesus had sinned in any way, He could not have been the sinless sacrifice that we needed to take away our sins.

This was exactly what Satan wanted to happen.

Notice that the only reason Jesus might have given Satan's offer any consideration at all was that He had seen—peeked, if you will—the kingdoms with His own eyes. It wouldn't have been nearly as strong a temptation if Satan had merely described to Jesus the kingdoms he proposed to give Him. A picture is worth a thousand words, and *temptation with a peek* is worth far more than temptation by description.

That is exactly why this play is so effective for Satan. Showing is always more effective and powerful than telling. We are constantly confronted with temptation through our eyes. The average American comes in contact with 30,000 advertisements per day. Now, "coming in contact" can mean lots of things. Simply flipping past an ad in a magazine could be considered coming in contact with it. If you read the newspaper, you could easily come in contact with twenty or thirty ads in just one section of the paper, even if you don't stop to read them. We see ads on billboards, buses, and bus stops. We see them on television, in movies, and at the store. Ads tend to work on the same premise as *temptation with a peek*. Many ads use *temptation with a promise* in conjunction with the peek. They tell us that *we can have* (a promise) *what we see* (a peek).

This works very well with selling "things"—cars, clothing, cosmetics, vacations, food—but it also works with selling us ideas. The behavior seen in television shows and movies shapes the way that we think. I've seen some studies claiming that more than 70% of teens say that their sexual behavior is influenced by what they see on television or in the movies.

It's incredibly dangerous to think that we're immune to such influences (see 1 Corinthians 10:12). That's like daydreaming while standing on defense, not paying attention to what's going on. If we're not paying attention we can't defend against the play—and by the time we know what's going on it could be too late. Touchdown—for the wrong side! Satan's temptations are exactly like that.

The pictures that we see—the things that we peek at—stay with us for a very long time, and they leave an imprint on our minds. In my early teens I went to camp at a Christian college in Wisconsin, and every week we heard a special speaker. I still remember quite a few of the speakers, and I remember a few of the lessons, too. One of the most powerful messages I ever heard there was on the verse in Proverbs that says "As a man thinketh, so is he" (Proverbs 23:7, KJV). The speaker was using music as an example, but the principle he addressed applies to other media. His point was that music paints pictures, and music holds pictures, and pictures last forever. If music paints pictures that remain, what about actual images in magazines, on the Internet, or in a movie? In his autobiography, comedian Tim Allen describes how he vividly remembers the first time he saw a naked woman—a poster in the bedroom of the older brother of his friend. Even though the incident had taken place many years earlier, he remembered the poster in incredible detail. Images stay with us, and that's why we have to be so careful.

This play is among those that Satan uses most. We're bombarded by opportunities to peek every day, because we live in a culture that flaunts the physical. For girls, especially, every act of selecting an outfit becomes a battle between modesty and indecency. Shirts seem to be getting tighter, lower from the top, and higher from the bottom, all at the same time. Girls, don't give guys glimpses they don't need to see! If you respect yourself, and if you want respect from guys, do everyone a favor by dressing modestly. Dannah Gresh and Hayley DiMarco do an excellent job of addressing this issue, and I would encourage you to read their books for more targeted advice on how to choose your wardrobe.[1]

To conclude, regardless of how prepared you are for it, you will be exposed to the *temptation with a peek.* The peek itself is not necessarily sin; Jesus got a peek of what Satan had to offer Him. Simply seeing it was not wrong, but yielding to the temptation would have been. Remember, a peek can be anything from something you would really like to own to someone you think is really attractive. Only when you dwell on the peek and think about it in an inappropriate way does it become a sin.

I believe it was Martin Luther put it like this: "You can't stop a bird from flying over your head, but you can stop it from making a nest in your hair." You'll see tempting things, and there is a limit to what you can do about it. (The so-called "black-and-blue Pharisees" tried going around blindfolded in the first century, but that didn't really stop them from sinning). What you *can* control is what you let your mind dwell on—which peeks you'll let "build a nest" in your hair. When you dwell on these things, you'll begin to covet or lust, and the Bible makes it very clear that both those things are sin. Jesus said that whoever looks on a woman to lust after her has committed adultery with her already in his heart. Guard your mind and keep it clear of wrong thoughts. Remember Paul's advice in Philippians 4:8—think on things that are good and pure.

---

1 Hayley DiMarco, *Sexy Girls: How Hot is Too Hot?* and Dannah Gresh, *Secret Keeper: The Delicate Power of Modesty.*

There's nothing wrong with seeing another person and thinking that he or she is attractive. It's when you allow your thoughts to go *beyond* "He's cute" or "She's pretty" that you get into trouble. Unless he or she is your husband or wife (and I certainly hope that you'll find your husband or wife attractive!), other thoughts about that attractive person are off limits for you. Make sure you're just admiring beauty and not desiring to physically possess that person.

Instant Replay

By virtue of the number of things and people that you get a peek at every day, *temptation with a peek* is one of the strongest attacks in Satan's playbook. The peek itself is not a sin, but it is often the gateway to a greater temptation—the temptation to covet something or someone that is not yours to have. Guard your mind diligently to ensure that you are not letting the temporary peeks turn into permanent problems.

Chapter 6

Play #6: Temptation with a Promise

I mentioned briefly in the last chapter that the entire advertising industry works on the premise of *temptation with a promise*. And advertising is exactly the business that Satan is in. Satan sells sin, and he often does it through advertising—presenting sin in slick packaging with a clever slogan, all accompanied by a wonderful promise.

Think of the last commercial you saw on TV or the last ad you saw in your favorite magazine. What was the point of the advertisement? To entice you to buy a product, based on the promise—explicit or implied—that doing so would provide something you need. It will make your teeth whiter, get a stain out of your favorite shirt, make you a better basketball player, or make all the girls or guys at school like you. Whatever the product is and whatever the form of the ad, there is a promise involved. If you try the products in question, it doesn't take long before you realize that they don't always live up to the promises made in the advertisements. Far worse than any shortcomings in a product, however, is the complete and utter failure—and inability—of sin to live up to the promises that Satan makes in his advertisements. *Temptation with a promise* is one of Satan's greatest offensive weapons.

In Matthew 4:9 Satan tells Jesus, "All these things I will give You if You will fall down and worship me." A promise! Satan promised Jesus that he would give Him "all these things" in exchange for a moment of worship. Satan promises something else to us—something far more realistic, pleasurable, and immediate: popularity or fame, fun or fortune, a really good feeling or instant happiness.

Maybe you've been tempted to cheat on a test or on a homework assignment. The "promise" from Satan in that case is a better grade or the absence of an unpleasant consequence (for failing or not turning in an assignment). Maybe you've been tempted to take a performance-enhancing drug. The promise in that case is better performance—a faster time, a longer home run, or a higher jump. Maybe you were tempted to steal. The promise then is the possession of something that you otherwise would not have had. The "promise" that accompanies temptation is the payoff, the reward, the goal.

Sometimes the promise is as simple as a thrill, a feeling of pleasure or escape. People quite often take things that don't belong to them simply for the excitement of doing so; they may not even want whatever it is that they take. These people steal for the same reason that other people go bungee jumping—the thrill. I don't know anyone who gets excited about strapping on a harness, or about signing legal waivers, or about the actual act of jumping off of a bridge. The only reason to do these things is for the thrill.

Many teens engage in sexual activity because they think it will feel good. They often have the act itself in mind, but long-range feelings may play a role as well—they may think sex will help them to feel more in love, or more grown up. Many teens also take drugs—drink them, snort them, smoke them, inject them—in order to "feel" something: perhaps less inhibited, less afraid, or less sad. What most of these reasons have in common is that the act itself is almost never the point. Many teens and young adults say that they don't even like the taste of beer, yet they drink it regularly because of the promise of fitting in, having fun, and so on. In short, the promise becomes the motivation.

In our passage from Matthew, Jesus was not tempted to worship Satan because worshiping Satan was somehow attractive. He was tempted to worship Satan because of the promise of what He would receive. The promise is dressed up, shined up, surrounded in neon lights and made to look as attractive as it possibly can. Why? Because that's the only way temptation, like sales, will work most of the time. Yet, as I mentioned in chapter 3 ("Temptation with Protection"), no one is ever tempted by the truth.

Imagine seeing an advertisement or a commercial that said, "Please buy our laundry detergent. Our entire company exists to make and sell laundry detergent, and the purpose of doing so is to make money. In reality, this detergent will clean your clothes about as well as the other detergents on the supermarket shelf. It won't make your clothes smell like spring because, frankly, no one can artificially create that smell. We changed the packaging to make it look a little more stylish. We added one ingredient so that we could call it a 'new formula.' We even put one extra scoop in the container so that we could say that it was 'larger than ever.' So, next time you need laundry detergent, please buy ours. Thanks."

Except for the fact that a few people who would be amused by its candor, this advertisement would be probably be ineffective. Why? Because facts are not usually appealing.

Most ads are all sizzle and no steak, but this ad is the reverse. And the same can be said of the temptations that we face every day.

How tempting would premarital sex be if the temptation included warnings about heartache, sexually transmitted diseases, and the possibility of pregnancy and childbirth? Most young people fall into temptation—sexual and otherwise—because they are blinded by the promises of pleasure, protection, and possibility. But the promise associated with most temptations is worthless—outright lies. It's about as reliable as the promise of good health associated with the elixirs sold by traveling medicine men in the Old West.

But what about the times when the promise seems to come true? After all, don't some laundry detergents really get the stains out better than others? Sure, there are times when the promise is at least partially true. For example, doing drugs or having sex might make you feel really good for a little while. Cheating on a test or a homework assignment might get you a better grade. Drinking until you pass out might help you forget your pain for a little while. Selling drugs might get you a lot of money. Stealing might get you something you wanted—something you didn't have the money to buy. But all of these things are only short-term payoffs.

The pleasure that comes with sin is short-lived. The Bible talks clearly about the "fleeting pleasures of sin" (Hebrews 11:25). It might feel really good, and it might even seem to solve all of your problems, but only for a little while. When the high goes away, you would have to take more drugs to feel the way you felt when you were feeling good. (This holds true for pornography, gambling, and other addictive behaviors as well). Having sex might feel really good at the moment, but when the act of sex takes place outside of marriage, without the emotional bonds that should exist first, that pleasant sensation will pass and will quite often be replaced by entirely different feelings. (For a biblical example that demonstrates this perfectly read the story of Amnon and Tamar in 2 Samuel 13). Cheating might get you a better grade this time, but since you didn't really master the material on your own, you will have to continue to cheat in order to maintain the grade that you got by cheating the first time. So the upside is very limited, and it's also short-term.

Satan is great at making things look good, but the reality is very much like an old movie set. From the front, or from a distance, it looks attractive, solid, and real. But when you get up close, when you open the door, or when you look from a different angle, you see that it's nothing but a façade, and that it's really nothing but a few two-by-fours holding up the false front. What looked so incredibly appealing is really worthless. That is the reality of temptation.

The only way to defend against *temptation with a promise* is to take the time to look deeper. Pause long enough to recognize the temptation for what it really is, or you'll be beaten every time.

Instant Replay

Satan is a master at presenting things with a positive spin and showing you all the wonderful things that can happen when you yield to temptation. What he never bothers to tell you, and what he doesn't want you to know, is that the fun part is short-lived, if it materializes at all. Any promise from Satan is just a trap. Look deeper to make sure you aren't the next sucker!

Chapter 7

Play #7: Temptation with Potential

As we have already discussed, most temptations seem to come with the potential for a huge payoff. *Temptation with potential* combines many of the features of other plays in Satan's playbook. In many ways "potential" is synonymous with "promise." We often see the potential for something on the other side of the temptation and get sucked into the promise that it could be ours. Jesus, in our text from Matthew, was confronted with the potential of having something to eat. He could command the stones to become bread. He was faced with the potential of becoming the ruler of all the kingdoms of the world; all He had to do was bow down and worship Satan. The "potential" is what we use to justify the sin. "Yes," we tell ourselves, "it's wrong, but if I do it this one time I'll get what I want."

Potential is a word that's used a lot in our culture. Promising young athletes are often touted as having a lot of "potential." The word is used in academics the same way, and in the arts, in business...in just about every area of life. Potential means that the possibility is there; it just hasn't yet become reality. It can be used to refer to positive things and to negative things. Many young athletes have the potential to improve their skills to become better players. Young musicians have the potential to become masters at their instruments. Conversely, someone who is unable or unwilling to control his anger has the potential to become very bad company, and someone who can't keep a secret has the potential to have few friends. The fact is, within all of us lies the potential to do horrible things. Scripture makes it clear that we're all sinners, that none of us is righteous in ourselves, and that we all have a sin nature—we are *born* sinners. Satan exploits that potential—that horrible, ugly potential—by presenting us with a slick, attractive promise related to something that we want.

Really, almost every temptation contains a bit of potential and almost every sin is an attempt to make the "potential" a reality. Just look at this very basic list of examples:

SIN	**POTENTIAL**
Cheating	Better grade
Shoplifting	Something for free
Drugs or alcohol	Feeling good
Bullying	Feeling superior

In these examples the temptation exists almost solely because of the potential. Cheating, in other words, is only tempting because of the temptation to get a better grade. Very few people cheat because it's fun, or because it gives them some sort of thrill. They cheat because they want a better grade than they are willing to work for. And unless shoplifting is some sort of gang initiation, most people who shoplift just want free stuff. The same is true of the other two instances.

Seldom, however, do we stop to consider the other kind of potential—the negative consequences. Let's look at that for a moment:

SIN	**POTENTIAL**
Cheating	Getting caught
Shoplifting	Getting caught
Drugs or alcohol	Addiction, family pain, jail, death
Bullying	Hurting someone else

Getting caught for cheating will result in disciplinary action at school: a failing grade on the assignment, and perhaps suspension or expulsion. Getting caught shoplifting can result in fines, court dates, being permanently banned from the store from which you stole, and even jail time. Of course all these things come with the potential for disciplinary action from your parents, as well as embarrassment and humiliation.

I've counseled many young people who have gotten themselves into trouble as a result of actions that lasted only a few short minutes. There are many people either dead or in prison because of a mistake made just once, or because of some wrong-headed action committed in anger. Kids have told me, "I just wasn't thinking." Caution and prudence are boring; life is a big adventure, they say, and the more fun you have, the better.

Well, that's true to an extent: Life is an adventure, and it's good to have fun. But God knows the potential (good and bad) of every decision we make. He's an expert in risk management. He knows how quickly something that looks like fun can turn into a disaster with long-lasting or even fatal consequences. For that very reason He has given us principles to live by. One of those principles is that we are to respect those who are in authority over us. Now, that's not always easy—very few people of any age enjoy being told what to do, and the vast majority of young people think that they know better than the adults in their lives do. (Come on, you know it's true!)

I have served in positions where I had to make and enforce a lot of rules. That can make me a less-than-popular guy. But the rules are all there for a good reason, regardless of how hard it is for kids to accept. One of the most difficult things for me to do is watch young people make decisions that I know will not turn out well. I've had dozens of conversations with young people in which I've carefully explained what the consequences of their choices could be, and how things have turned out for others who have made the very same decision. But almost every one of them says, "That won't happen to me." They buy into Satan's *temptation with protection* and *temptation with potential* and are blinded to the negative potential of their course of action because the positive potential looks so glittering.

Not too long ago I had a conversation with a 17-year-old girl who wanted to make some decisions for her future that I didn't think were wise. She outlined all the reasons why she thought it was a good idea to do things her way. I acknowledged that if everything worked out exactly the way she wanted it to, her plan could succeed. But then I asked her to think about all the things that could go wrong if even one step of her plan went awry. She listened. And then she told me that she *knew* things would work out fine.

So I followed up with this crucial point, which I believe is the heart of the matter: waiting on God versus instant gratification. "If you do it the way you want to, and it works out, that will be great. But consider what *could* go wrong.

If you do it the way I'm suggesting, you will still end up with everything that you want based on your plan, but on a slightly different timetable."

Instant gratification, so exemplified by our culture, is a huge plus for Satan in his *temptation with potential* play. We allow ourselves to be suckered into believing that if we cut a few corners here or there (*if* we take out loans instead of saving money, *if* we are discreet about sin so that no one will get hurt—there's always an "if" involved), then everything will be okay. We convince ourselves that the "ifs" will always come out in our favor, that we'll be able to get exactly what we want when we want it, and that we know better than anyone else advising us.

Sometimes, against all odds, things do work out the way we want them to, and the potential that we were tempted with becomes a reality. Perhaps we get away with cutting corners, we're able to pay off the loan, for example, or we're able to keep that secret sin a secret. However, the painful truth is that, in most cases, this is the worst thing that could ever happen: overconfidence can be the result, and overconfidence means that we're more likely to take another risk in the future. And usually the risks get bigger as we go along.

Let's be very clear here: Potential is a word that gets used a lot, and it's used quite often in reference to young people. Potential in itself is not a bad thing; every human being has potential of one kind or another. However, few people ever live up to their potential, either because they tire of the work involved or they tire of the opposition that they must overcome. One of the saddest things that can happen to a person is to realize that he has not fulfilled his own potential. God doesn't want that to happen to you! It's only when Satan uses potential to tempt us to take short cuts, or to do things that we know we shouldn't do, that potential becomes a pitfall.

Knowing God's will for your life is, in some ways, very simple. The Scriptures make it very clear that it is God's will for everyone to love God and to love others. Those, as Jesus said, are the two greatest commandments. There are plenty of other instructions in the Bible that apply to everyone, and obeying those things is God's will for your life, my life, and the life of every believer.

On the other hand, knowing God's specific will for your life can be very difficult. There is no magic formula in the Bible for which career path God wants you to follow, what college He may want you to attend, or what person He may want you to marry—and the list goes on.

This is where *temptation with potential* can be very dangerous. You have some of your own ideas about what you'd like to do with your life, where you might like to go to college, and what kind of person you'd like to marry. There is nothing wrong with that, unless, of course, your designs for those things are based on fleshly desires or worldly influences. The book of James warns us that our prayers can go unanswered because we ask for things to "spend them on our passions" (James 4:3). In other words, we ask for things out of selfishness and greed, not out of a humble spirit, a desire to help others, or a desire to serve God. If I spend time praying for a Porsche, it's unlikely that my prayer will be answered anytime soon: not only do I not need a Porsche, but buying one would require me to divert money that I could be spending on other (more meaningful) things.

That's where Satan comes in. Through the influences of the world, he plants ideas in our minds about what kind of clothes we *need* to wear, what kind of cars we *should* drive, what kind of boyfriend, or girlfriend, or spouse we *deserve* to have, and how much money we are *supposed* to make.

Ninety-nine percent of the time, though, the world's goals and desires are contrary to God's word and His will. But Satan doesn't care; in fact, that's exactly what he wants. And he then uses *temptation with potential* to convince us that we could easily have those things. Satan convinces us that if we just cut one corner or fudge the truth about one thing, *presto,* our "potential" has been realized and we suddenly have exactly what we thought we wanted. But here's the reality: We often confuse our needs and our wants, and what we think we want seldom brings us the happiness we think it will. As soon as we get what we want, there's something else just beyond our reach. Underline this, highlight it, write it on a card, and tape it to your mirror—remember it somehow: *There will always be "something else."*

Someone has wisely said, "There is often less danger in the things we fear than in the things we desire." Far too often the one thing we want the most is indeed dangerous. It may be dangerous because of our lusts, as James said. It may distract us from doing (or wanting) things that are more important. And it may be dangerous because when we do get it (whatever "it" is), that "success" will feed into Satan's plan and we'll be much more likely to fall for the *temptation with potential* next time. So be aware of wanting anything too much, and regularly check your mental "wish list" to see if the things you want are really things you should be pursuing.

Satan is also very good at convincing us that what we want is also God's will for our lives. He's adept at fooling us into thinking that if a certain path worked out for us, then it must have been God's will. Be careful of that assumption!

This is illustrated by the account of the man who had been successfully dieting for some time. He had trimmed down and had really gotten better about not eating too much junk food. But he had a weakness for hot Krispy

Kreme donuts, and one day as he was driving along he saw the Krispy Kreme sign up ahead. His mouth began to water and he suddenly craved a hot, sticky donut. "Maybe this is God's reward to me for being so good for so long," he reasoned. "If the 'HOT' light is on when I go by, it must be God's will for me to have a hot Krispy Kreme donut." And wouldn't you know it, by the time the guy had made his third trip around the block, the HOT light was on!

Every one of us is that guy. We set our minds and hearts on something that *we* want—not that God wants for us—and then we set about trying to make it happen. We try and try and try until eventually we make it a reality, and then we convince ourselves that since the plan worked, it must have been God's will for us. Not at all!

Instant Replay

Satan tempted Jesus with the potential of having something to eat, the potential of owning and ruling over the entire world, and the potential of enjoying the world's first amusement-park-style plunge by jumping off of the pinnacle of the temple and having angels ensure a soft landing. But Jesus knew Satan's playbook, and He didn't buy this pitch.

Similarly, Satan uses worldly influences like TV, music, movies, and the Internet to put ideas in your head of things that look or sound good to you. He tries to convince you that you deserve these things, and that they could easily be yours if you simply do things the way he has suggested. If the choice you're faced with will enable you to get something that you really want (or think you want), but that won't please God, you're facing *temptation with potential.* Be on the lookout for it, keep your defenses up, and stop letting Satan beat you with that play!

Now the serpent was more crafty than any other beast of the field that the Lord God had made.

He said to the woman, "Did God actually say, 'You shall not eat of any tree in the garden'?" And the woman said to the serpent, "We may eat of the fruit of the trees in the garden, but God said, 'You shall not eat of the fruit of the tree that is in the midst of the garden, neither shall you touch it, lest you die.'" But the serpent said to the woman, "You will not surely die. For God knows that when you eat of it your eyes will be opened, and you will be like God, knowing good and evil." So when the woman saw that the tree was good for food, and that it was a delight to the eyes, and that the tree was to be desired to make one wise, she took of its fruit and ate, and she also gave some to her husband who was with her, and he ate. Then the eyes of both were opened, and they knew that they were naked. And they sewed fig leaves together and made themselves loincloths.

Genesis 3:1-7

Chapter 8

Run It Again!

A successful football coach develops plays for his offense, and when he finds a play that works he continues to run that play for as long as it's successful. If a play doesn't work a successful coach will take it out of the playbook. After all, a coach's success is measured by wins and losses, so he needs plays that gain yards for the offense and result in touchdowns—and victories.

Satan's successes can be measured in wins and losses, too, in a manner of speaking. When we humans give in to temptation, he wins, and we lose. By that metric, Satan is incredibly successful—far more successful than any coach for any sport ever. In fact, the plays that we have looked at in this book are so successful that Satan has been running them since his very first game, and is still successfully using them today.

The first seven verses of Genesis 3, printed just before this chapter, is a very well-known part of the Bible. These few short verses changed the entire course of history. Prior to these verses, everything was perfect, because there was no sin. When Eve yielded to temptation, however, and ate the fruit of the tree of the knowledge of good and evil—and when Adam ate after her—sin entered the world. And every human being since, including you and me, has been guilty of sin.

Let's walk through this very first game of good versus evil—Satan's first attempts at running the plays in his playbook.

Temptation with Perversion

Right away in Genesis 3:1 we see that Satan perverts, or twists, what God had told Adam and Eve. He implies that God is not good or fair because He is withholding something good from Adam and Eve. Satan asks Eve, "Did God *actually* say..." (emphasis mine). We can almost hear the inflection of Satan's voice in these words—probably because we've done the same thing on numerous occasions. When we try to justify something that we know is wrong, we look for any little crack, any bit of wiggle room, that will support our position. Satan is speaking very sarcastically here, using words and tone to imply a distrust of God's instruction. More than likely you've either said this yourself or heard your friends say it: "Did your parents *actually* say that you can't go to the party?" or "Your dad *really* won't let you go to the concert?" or "Your mom *seriously* said you aren't allowed to watch that?"

In each of these instances the underlying assertion in the italicized words is something akin to: "Are you kidding me?!?" Sure, parties, concerts, and movies can be fun—great ways to spend time with friends and to make new friends. So when moms and dads establish a boundary and say that a certain party or concert or movie is off limits, we immediately try to figure out a way of perverting or twisting what they said so that we can do it anyway.

Of course, the odds are good that your parents never said that all parties, concerts, and movies are off limits. Certainly mine never said that! Similarly, God never told Adam and Eve that all types of fruit in the garden were off limits to them. On the contrary, He allowed them free access to all the fruit they wanted, saying only that *one* tree in the garden was off limits. He did that because He knew better than Adam and Eve what was good and wholesome and appropriate, and He wanted to protect them, not because He wanted to deprive them of any pleasure.

Parents and other authority figures usually make their rules and boundaries for the same reason. Like Adam and Eve, though, teens can be easily suckered into thinking that, despite all the things they *can* do—all of the concerts, the parties, and the movies that are allowed—the most fun will take place at the ones they miss. All of the fruit we can eat, in other words, pales in comparison with the fruit that's off limits. It seems we always want what we can't have.

Therefore, it doesn't take much for believers to fall into this temptation. We're quick to assume that there was some misunderstanding, that what we thought we heard was not really what was meant, because there's no way that our parents would knowingly prohibit us from having so much fun. To get what we want, we're more than happy to twist and pervert the boundaries that parents have established.

This happens with boundaries that God has put in place, too.

God says that sex outside of marriage (which includes sex before marriage) is sin, plain and simple. But we twist that by convincing ourselves that when there is *love* premarital sex is not wrong. Cheating is a form of stealing, and God certainly says that stealing is sin, but we may tell ourselves that a good test grade is really important and that we really couldn't study because we were too busy. It can't possibly be *that* big a deal to look at someone else's paper to get one or two answers—right?

In short, when we yield to *temptation with perversion* we twist the truth, or buy into a twisted truth, so that we can get what we want.

Temptation with Protection

Next, in Genesis 3:4, we see *temptation with protection.* Eve answers Satan by telling him that if she or Adam eat the fruit of the tree, they will die. (Eve even throws in the idea that she and Adam will die if they merely touch the tree, though the Bible doesn't indicate that God prohibited them from touching it). Now, the death of which God warned them was both physical and spiritual death. Up to this point, Adam and Eve were sinless and able to live forever, both physically and spiritually. By eating that fruit, however, they became guilty of violating God's instruction, and thereby guilty of sin. The consequence of sin is both spiritual death (because sinners are no longer capable of a right relationship with God) and physical death (because sin will result in the deterioration of the physical body, ultimately resulting in death).

Satan does not even hesitate, though, before he tempts Eve with protection. "You will not surely die," he tells Eve. Sound familiar? In Matthew 4, remember, Satan tells Jesus that if He will cast Himself off the pinnacle of the temple He will be protected by angels. Here, Satan tells Eve that she will not die, that eating the fruit will not result in death, and that God had just told them about death because He did not want them to have the knowledge that He did.

I discussed earlier how we're often tempted to do something by the assurance that we aren't going to get hurt. Despite oft-repeated warnings, we are convinced that "it" will not happen to us. Adam had received the instruction directly from God Himself—*eat anything you want except the fruit of this tree, because if you do, you will die.* Eve didn't hear it from God directly, but Adam had obviously told her about it—and perhaps, to be on the safe side, Adam had added the "don't even touch it" admonition that Eve relayed to Satan.

Temptation with Prevarication

We also see in verse 4 another of Satan's favorite plays—one we have not previously analyzed. Let's call it *temptation with prevarication*, a ten-dollar word that simply means "lie." Satan lied to Eve when he told her that she would not die. He knew he was lying, but he did it anyway, because Satan has no regard for the truth. His only objective is to win—and when we sin, he wins.

Lying, to Satan, is simply a means to an end. "All's fair in love and war," the old expression goes. And although athletic contests are sometimes referred to as "doing battle," life really is a battle—a spiritual battle. And Satan uses any tactic that might be effective. There is no Geneva Convention-type document when it comes to spiritual warfare, nothing that defines the fair and decent way the two sides must behave. Satan and his forces attack with no-holds-barred determination. So lying is just one more means of enticing us to sin.

Temptation with a Promise

Satan tempts Eve with the promise that if she eats the fruit her eyes will be opened and she will be like God, knowing good and evil. Satan's temptation is always accompanied by a promise of some great reward or benefit—something that makes us believe that yielding to the temptation will definitely be worth it. In this particular case, Adam and Eve did know good and evil after they ate the fruit. They also experienced immediate spiritual death and the beginnings of what would eventually become physical death. (Satan, of course, conveniently failed to mention anything about that). And the way Adam and Eve knew good and evil—and that you and I know good and evil—is nothing like the way that God knows good and evil. God is perfect and holy; He never thinks evil thoughts or engages in evil behavior. Adam and Eve—and every human being since—did both.

I once taught my daughter about this principle at lunch. Then six, she had done something that she knew she shouldn't do. After being admonished, she just replied, "But it's fun." My daughter had already firmly engaged *temptation with a promise*. The pleasure that she derived from engaging in that wrong behavior made it worth it, in her eyes. The behavior in question was really rather harmless—a question of good manners versus bad. With Satan, however, the behaviors and thoughts he tempts with are seldom harmless, and the benefit or "fun" that he promises is never worth it in the long run. I told my young daughter that fun is never an excuse for doing something we shouldn't do. We should always strive to do what is right, even if, at the moment, we feel doing so will cost us some enjoyment.

Temptation with Potential

In Genesis 3:6, we see that when Eve looked at the tree and its fruit, it was "a delight to the eyes, and…to be desired to make one wise." Herein lies the potential—*to become wise*. Eve believed that Satan was telling the truth and that if she simply ate the fruit she would become wise. She would become like God! Is there any greater potential than that?

Now, was there anything wrong with Eve's desiring to be wise? Certainly not. Solomon asked God for wisdom, and God was so pleased with his request that He gave Solomon wisdom, land, and riches. Scripture is full of instruction on the importance of wisdom and the peril of foolishness. God wants us to be wise. The problem in this instance was that Eve was going about it in the wrong way. Satan does this frequently—he will use something that is good and decent and right to entice us to do something wrong.

Is there anything wrong with wanting to get good grades? No. But when you're tempted to cheat or plagiarize because of the potential that you see for getting good grades without work, you're trying to obtain a good thing in the wrong way. Is there anything wrong with wanting to be accepted or loved? No way. But when you're tempted to engage in inappropriate or even illegal behavior because you see the potential for acceptance or love, you are again trying to obtain a good thing in the wrong way.

For Adam and Eve there was a right way to obtain wisdom, but eating the forbidden fruit was the wrong way. So the sin was not what Eve *wanted*, but what Eve *did*. The ends don't justify the means, and they never will, as long as those "means" are sinful. We can't honor God by disobeying Him.

Temptation with the Possible

Finally, we see in verse 6 that Eve, and then Adam, yielded to *temptation with the possible.* All Eve had to do was reach up and pick the fruit off the tree. Nothing to it—she didn't even need a ladder! Eve gave the fruit to Adam, and he ate it, too—hand delivered. So remember, we will almost always be tempted by things that are possible for us. *Every* serious temptation that you or I will face could accurately be placed under the heading of *temptation with the possible.* Every one of those temptations could also be accurately filed under at least one of the other temptations that have been discussed.

There are many other plays in Satan's playbook—*temptation with pleasure, temptation by peer pressure*, and so on—but by now you get the idea: Satan hasn't developed any new strategies in a long time. He's developed new ways of delivering them and new disguises for them to wear, but the temptations ultimately are the same. Notice that what could be called Satan's two biggest temptations ever—his temptation of Adam and Eve in the Garden of Eden and his temptation of Christ in the wilderness—used identical game plans. There is really only one crucial difference: Adam and Eve yielded to temptation; Jesus Christ did not.

Chapter 9

Preparing for Battle

We've now seen Satan's playbook. However, knowing your enemy is not the only necessary ingredient for success in battling temptation. If, in football, you got the playbook of your opponent, would you win the game just by knowing what plays the other team was going to run? Knowing the plays would do you no good whatsoever unless you knew how to defend against them.

Every great football team has an offensive playbook, but it also has defensive strategies that are developed to defend against specific plays. If the head coach of a football team knows what offensive plays the opponent will run in the next game, he and his defensive coordinator will spend the majority of their time preparing their defense to counter those plays. The more effective the defense, the fewer plays the opposition will be able to run, and the sooner their own offense will take the field.

So, once we know the plays in Satan's playbook, we must use this information to develop our defense. Since our defense is truth, knowing the truth is preparation for doing battle with the enemy.

Go back to Matthew 4 and look at verses 4, 5, 7, and 10. The phrase "It is written" is repeated in all four verses. Why? Because Jesus used Scripture to defeat Satan. The defense that Jesus Himself employed when He was tempted by Satan was quoting Scripture!

Don't think, "Well sure, that's easy for Him to do; Jesus knew all of Scripture and could recite any of it any time with ease. I can't do that." While it's true that Jesus knew all Scripture, He used just four verses from the book of Deuteronomy to defend against Satan's attacks. Anyone can memorize four verses!

The key in a successful defensive scheme in football is knowing which defense to use and when to use it, and then executing it exactly as practiced. Similarly, it's not enough in spiritual battle to know that something helpful is in the Bible somewhere. To be successful, we have to really *know* the truth. When temptation comes, we will seldom, if ever, have the opportunity (or the inclination) to go look up what the Bible has to say about it. In any setting in which two opponents are facing each other, the key to success is catching the opponent off guard.

In football you'll often see a quarterback hit a wide-open receiver for an easy touchdown. How does that happen? In football vernacular, it happens when someone on defense blows the coverage. That means at least one person on defense did not fulfill his responsibility. He may have read the offense wrong (so he was expecting a different play); he may have been fooled by a fake or a decoy; or he may simply have missed his man. Regardless, because he was not where he was supposed to be, the offense scored an easy touchdown. The alert attacker will always exploit the defender's errors or lack of preparation. What does *not* happen when the wide receiver finds himself wide open downfield is this: He will never call out to the man who is supposed to be defending him, alerting him to the fact that he's wide open and inviting the defender to catch up.

You could apply this principle to a variety of settings. Think of medieval times: If one knight has left his sword and armor by a tree while he frolics in a stream and waters his horse, he has left himself vulnerable to attack. If his opponent arrives at that moment, what do you think would happen to the foolish knight? Never forget that in a real battle—including a spiritual battle—there is no such thing as a time-out. We must be prepared when the fight arrives.

You may remember that several years ago it was trendy to wear a bracelet with the letters W.W.J.D., which stood for "What Would Jesus Do?" These bracelets were everywhere. And although the idea behind this movement was a good one, the bracelet's true meaning seemed lost on most of the people wearing it, many of whom might not have known what Jesus' course of action in a given situation was likely to be. Remember, there are no time-outs: you need to know what Jesus would do *before* you are confronted with temptation. Take the time to find pertinent Bible passages before temptation comes; then, memorize the verses, or at least know the principles involved.

You may wonder how to locate relevant Bible verses. There are many resources for finding Scripture: Web sites, concordances, Bible indexes, and so on. I suggest that you take time, right now, to make a list of the five or six things that are the biggest sources of temptation for you. (They will be different for each believer). Then, using one of the resources mentioned above, or other resources available to you, look up Bible verses that address those issues. (There is a list of verses at the back of this book that you may find helpful for getting started, but this list is by no means exhaustive). Then write out the verses that are most applicable on an index card and try to memorize them—at least one verse for each of your main sources of temptation. When you find yourself confronted with the temptation, recite the Scripture to yourself, out loud if need be. Maybe you could even encourage your youth pastor to do this with your youth group—that is, identify sources of temptation and the Bible passages that are relevant to battling them.

What happens when a football team deploys its defense effectively against an offensive attack? The offense is shut down. In football, that means that after three plays the offense will punt and the defense will get the ball back—enabling their team to go on offense! In spiritual warfare, when we defend ourselves successfully against Satan's attacks, he will flee. Jesus knew the truth, and He used it to defend Himself effectively against Satan's temptations, and Satan, defeated, left (Matthew 4:11). Satan, the father of lies, has no defense against truth.

The same can be true for us, too. The Bible says, in James 4:7, that if we resist the devil, he will flee from us. He won't just leave, he'll run away! If we're prepared to do battle, and we stick to our defensive game plan, we will have victory over Satan every time.

There is, however, one catch. It doesn't do us any good to know the playbook if we aren't on the team. If someone sitting in the stands at a football game knows every play the offense will run and exactly how the defense should set up, that information is useless because the spectator is not in a position to utilize the information that he possesses. He's not in the game. When it comes to confronting Satan's temptations, we're all in the game; no one is on the sidelines. But there's more to knowing the truth than what I've described in these few pages. Yes, you can defend against Satan's playbook—provided you are on the team.

You have to know the truth (the factual and Scriptural defenses against Satan's lies), and you also have to know the Truth (that is, Jesus Christ). Jesus said in John14:6 that He is "the way, the truth and the life."

If you've accepted Christ as your Savior, then you're on His team, and He's now your coach. He wants to develop a relationship with you, and He wants to provide you with everything you need to defend against Satan's attacks. He will be right there with you every step of the way, and He will bring to mind the Scriptures you've learned that apply to the temptations you will face. Take the principles in this book, combine them with a growing and maturing relationship with Christ, and you'll be victorious in your battle with Satan. Not every time, because you're still a sinner, and everyone continues to sin. But failures will become far less frequent. The difference is whether sin, or Christ, occupies the throne in your hearts.

Just as a football player revels in the thrill of victory on the field, you'll experience joy and excitement over the defeat of Satan's temptations. I hope that this book is helpful in preparing you for battle.

Before I close, though, I need point out that if you've never accepted Christ as your personal Savior, you're not on His team. You're in the game, because we all are, but you have no defensive strategy. Even though you now know the plays in Satan's playbook, you won't be able to defend against them because you have no coach and no teammates—you have only your own strength, and that's not enough.

If this describes you, please take the time to read the Appendix; it will explain how you can join Jesus' team. And that will be the best and most important decision you will ever make.

Appendix

Joining the Team

Unless you've accepted Jesus Christ as your Lord and Savior, the principles contained in this book won't help you much at all. You'll never be on the winning team, because the only way to be on that team is to accept Christ.

Although I'm continuing the football team analogy, accepting Christ is far more than joining a team. It's joining a family. It's also the most important decision that you'll ever make, because it will determine your future, both in this world and in eternity.

The Bible makes it very clear that ever since Adam and Eve yielded to temptation in the Garden of Eden every human being has been born a sinner. Romans 3:23 states very plainly that all have sinned. God is a righteous God, and He cannot allow sin in His presence or in His heaven. Yet, He's a loving God—and that's why He created Adam and Eve, and you and me, and every other human, with free will, so that we could decide for ourselves whether or not we wish to be in a relationship with Him. God could have chosen to compel our love, but forced love isn't really love, is it? Instead, He creates each person with the freedom to make his or her own decision about Him.

God desires a relationship with each person He has created. It was for that reason that He sent His Son, Jesus Christ, to pay the penalty for sin. And what was that penalty? Death. Romans 6:23 tells us that the wages of sin—the earned reward—is death. And since we're all guilty of sin, we're all equally deserving of death. But John 3:16 tells us that God loved the world—and each person in the world—so much that He sent His Son to die, so that anyone who accepts the gift of salvation, made possible through Christ's atoning death, might have eternal life. There is nothing that anyone can do to work his way into heaven or to deserve forgiveness of sins. There is one way, and only one way, to obtain forgiveness, and that is to accept Christ.

One effective way to understand God's offer of salvation through Christ is to simply examine the passages of Scripture that clearly reveal our need for salvation and God's plan for it. The text of the verses is provided here, along with the references, but I would encourage you to get a Bible and read them there, too, as well as the verses around them (the context) and other Bible passages. I would also encourage you to talk with a parent, friend, teacher, youth pastor, or other person who has accepted Christ. He or she will be able to answer questions you may have and will surely want to celebrate with you if you choose to accept Christ as your Savior. You may decide that you would like to have someone with you when you pray to ask forgiveness and accept Christ. There is a sample prayer at the end of the Scripture passages below, but there is nothing magical about it; it's not a formula. It's simply one example of how you might pray. The words themselves are not important. What is important is that you're sincere in your heart about accepting Jesus' sacrifice for you—and about turning your life over to Him.

Last, salvation is not a one-time thing. It is in the sense that you'll be saved instantly and permanently if you sincerely ask Christ to be your Savior, but it's not just a "get out of hell free" card. It's a decision that will have meaning and impact for the rest of your life. You'll be growing and maturing in your relationship with Christ for as long as you live. And Satan will not just go away because you join God's team. In fact, he may step up his efforts to tempt you, in order to discourage you or to destroy your witness to others. That's why it's so important to continue to study the Bible, to get involved in a Bible-teaching local church, and to remember the principles in this book.

All Humans are Sinners

"As it is written, none is righteous, no not one." Romans 3:10

"For all have sinned and fall short of the glory of God." Romans 3:23

"For the wages of sin is death…." Romans 6:23a

All Must Repent of Sin

"Repent therefore…that your sins may be blotted out." Acts 3:19

"If we confess our sins, He is faithful and just to forgive us our sins and to cleanse us from all unrighteousness." 1 John 1:9

All Must Accept Christ

"But God shows his love for us in that while we were still sinners, Christ died for us." Romans 5:8

"...but the free gift of God is eternal life in Christ Jesus our Lord." Romans 6:23b

"Because, if you confess with your mouth that Jesus is Lord and believe in your heart that God raised Him from the dead, you will be saved. For with the heart one believes and is justified, and with the mouth one confesses and is saved." Romans 10:9-10

A Sample Prayer

God in Heaven, I know I am a sinner. I cannot keep Your commands, and I am not worthy to enter heaven. I know that there is nothing that I can do on my own to obtain Your forgiveness. But I believe that Your Son Jesus died on the cross for my sins, that He rose again three days later, and that He lives now in Heaven with You. Please forgive me, cleanse my heart, and fill me with Your Spirit so that I might live my life for You. Thank You for loving me. Amen.

Scripture Reference Guide

General principles regarding thoughts
Proverbs 23:7
1 Corinthians 6:12
Philippians 4:8

Alcohol, Drug Abuse
Proverbs 20:1
Proverbs 23:19-20
Luke 21:34
Romans 12:1
1 Corinthians 6:19-20
Galatians 5:16
Ephesians 5:18
1 Thessalonians 5:16
1 Peter 1:13
1 Peter 5:8

Body Image
Psalm 139:14
Proverbs 25:16
Proverbs 31:30
Philippians 2:3

Communication
(This includes lying, gossiping, etc.)
Exodus 20:16
Psalm 19:4
Psalm 141:3
Proverbs 8:6-8
Proverbs 12:18
Proverbs 12:22
Proverbs 26:20
Ephesians 4:25
Ephesians 4:29
James 3:1-12

Coveting
Ecclesiastes 5:10-11
Matthew 6:19-21
Matthew 6:24
Luke 12:15
Colossians 3:1-3
Colossians 3:5
1 Timothy 6:6-10
Hebrews 13:5

Gambling
Luke 12:15
Luke 12:42
Philippians 2:4
1 Timothy 6:9-10a

Homosexuality
Leviticus 18:22
Romans 1:26-27

Lust
Matthew 5:27-28
Romans 13:14
Galatians 5:16-18
Colossians 3:5-7
Titus 2:11-12
1 Peter 1:14-16
1 Peter 2:11

Pornography
Proverbs 4:23
Matthew 5:28
Colossians 3:5

Selfishness, Self-centeredness
Matthew 20:26-28
1 Corinthians 10:24
1 Corinthians 13:5
Philippians 2:3-5
James 3:14-16

Sexual Activity
Galatians 5:16
Ephesians 4:22-23
1 Corinthians 6:15
1 Thessalonians 4:3-6
Hebrews 13:4

Temptation
Proverbs 1:10
2 Corinthians 11:14-15
James 4:7
1 Peter 5:8-9

About the Author

Jason Watson has been married to Kristina since 1999 and they have a son and a daughter. Jason earned his undergraduate degree in Political Science from Drake University, and has earned a Th.M. from Christian Bible College, a M.Ed. in Educational Leadership from Lynchburg College, and a M.A. in Biblical Studies, emphasis in Christian Education, from Trinity Theological Seminary. He has three years of Christian school teaching experience, having taught history, geography, government and economics in grades 6-12, and he has eight and a half years of administrative leadership experience in a Christian non-profit ministry (including five-and-a-half as CEO) providing residential group home placement for at-risk youth and Christian counseling to individuals, couples and families in the greater Lynchburg, VA area. He served as Headmaster of a small Christian school before he and his wife founded Lighthouse Academy in 2011, a private school providing education that is biblical in worldview and classical in structure.

Jason loves to learn and to teach, and considers himself privileged to have been given the opportunity to serve alongside some wonderful individuals in ministering to young people. It is certainly true that the teacher learns far more in preparing to teach than he can ever have time to teach, and Jason is grateful for all that he has learned in preparing to teach others. Most of all he is grateful for the lasting relationships that he has with former colleagues, students and residents.

CPSIA information can be obtained at www.ICGtesting.com
Printed in the USA
LVOW101320090513

333057LV00001B/11/P